# The Trouble with Golf

Written & illustrated by

**Garrick Tremain**

**David Bateman**

# Contents

# From the Artist

The golfer and the artist share one thing in common.

They face, in one case, an inviting fairway and, in the other, an unspoiled canvas: optimism is rampant, failure the remotest of possibilities. But soon, as each stroke fails to meet their high expectations, disappointment becomes dismay and finally despair.

Crestfallen to the point of contemplating abandonment, they suddenly and inexplicably find a stroke going exactly as foreseen. Spirits rise! They exalt in the delusion that they have suddenly "cracked it", and with enthusiasm rekindled they plunge onwards into the next series of catastrophes.

Why do we do it? Why are just two good strokes in the last nine holes sufficient to bring us back for one hundred bad ones the following week?

Millions play the game. A select few play it very well indeed. The rest of us suspect that with another round or two behind us we could be numbered amongst them.

# A Letter to Padraig

Dear Padraig Harrington,
I've seen you on TV.
Watched you winning tournaments
but know you've not seen me.

When everybody's making such
a fuss of Tiger Woods,
I always say (ask the wife)
"That Padraig! He's the goods!"

For several years I've idolised
your fortune and your fame,
and wonder if you'd drop a note
with hints to help my game.

'Tis not too much to ask I hope,
you really are the best...
I've just enclosed an envelope
stamped and self-addressed.

I think of you as champ-of-champs
and also as a friend
(on second thoughts let's hope the
stamps are okay from your end).

And Padraig, don't concern yourself,
I'm not the kind of jerk
who'll pinch your game and go on tour...
I can't get time off work.

# A Golfing Tip

It helps to keep one's game on track
and iron out all the kinks,
if every time one hits the ball
one concentrates and thinks,
the one who makes the biggest score
getting 'round the links,
is the one back in the clubhouse
who has to buy the drinks.

WHEN LEE'S BEEN SETTLING UP FOR AIR SHOTS
I'LL BET MRS WESTWOOD'S A BIT MORE REASONABLE!

# Achievements

When man can make a spaceship
that takes him to the moon,
an electronic organ
that always stays in tune.
When man can make an antidote
for every known disease,
cellphones that take photographs,
plastic hips and knees.

Make pills to spice your love life
when you're old and grey,
cameras that clock driving speed
from bloody miles away.
When man makes things that tell the sex
of babies still unborn,
makes maps of all the ocean floors
and does it with a yawn.

How can man – please tell me –
it's really got me beat...
get so excited if he makes
a putt of seven feet?

# All Your Own Doing

If, upon your opening shot,
you feel the bubble burst,
your optimism vanishing
halfway down the first.
If your ball goes bouncing
out of bounds instead of in,
you climb the fence to find it,
stripping raw meat from your shin.

If your ball plugs in the sand
you know it isn't fair,
someone moved the bunker
while your ball was in the air.
The keeper's left the mowers out,
your ball runs underneath.
You'd love to have a word with him
but can't unclench your teeth.

It says that in a straight line
the green's a hundred yards.
You know for you a straight line
is never on the cards.
You didn't bring wet weather gear,
they didn't forecast rain,
but should've 'cos you played the ninth,
waist-deep along the drain.

If the only time you hit a shot
that's any good at all,
is the moment you discover
you've played your partner's ball.
If they say, "You're in a hazard,
don't ground your club, old chap,"
and you wish that you knew someone
who'd grind it up for scrap.

If you've torn your brand-new trousers
while up a hawthorn hedge
you've climbed to see the fairway
or recover your new wedge.
If rabbit scrapes and divots are
your golf ball's choice of holes,
you've only got yourself to blame...

you should've gone to bowls.

Knowing in advance if we were
going to play well or badly
would save us untold grief, an
enormous amount of time and
countless balls.

# Bruce

Bunker play's a special skill
which Bruce had never mastered;
with sand iron he'd address the ball
"Righto, you little bastard!"

In clouds of dust and language
ten minutes could well pass,
with Bruce and ball still in the pot,
the sand out on the grass.

Despite his best endeavours,
thrashing all about,
hunger and exhaustion
would finally drive him out.

"I'm not one bit surprised," said Bruce.
"Indeed, can comprehend,
how it was in one of these
that Hitler met his end!"

13

# The Loyal & Ancient

Four geriatric golfers
played twice a week or so,
and always wondered secretly
who'd be first to go.

Onto the green stepped Archie,
at this point still alive,
but as he stooped to tee his ball
before he made his drive,
he suddenly lost balance
and couldn't catch his breath;
staggered wildly sideways
as white and cold as death.

He trembled as his eyeballs
rolled backward in their sockets;
tees and coins and markers
spewed out of his pockets.

As he lay there prostrate,
gasping on the tee,
through spittle meekly whispered,
"From now, lads, you're a three!"

The others shuffled forward,
as each one shook his hand,
said, "What a great stroke, Archie,"
and he died a happy man.

# McWhirter

McWhirter who played at Royal Scone,

took divots and carted them home,

then sewed them together

with sawgrass and heather,

and now has a course of his own.

# Beryl

Beryl loves her Tuesdays,
depending on the weather.
It's when the ladies congregate
and all play golf together.

It's social interaction
in the great outdoors.
A chance to tone their figures
and exercise their jaws.

Despite the mad frustrations
of air shots and lost balls,
it makes a break from baking cakes
and washing Bernie's smalls.

# Darryl

Darryl was an optimist
and often heard to say,
"I know I've got it in me –
I'll shoot my age one day!"

He would have done it by a stroke
last Thursday afternoon.
Timing was the problem...
he'd teed off years too soon.

When I was young
I could get quite upset
at the expense of
losing a new ball.
Today my dismay is
that I can't hit one
far enough to lose it.

# Cops & Robbers

Caught in the act by a cop,
robbing his local golf shop,
he attempted to bolt,
the cop cried out, "Halt!"
and shot him to get him to stop.

Said the judge, "While this chap in his prime
was committing a serious crime,
I cannot concede
there was any need
to shoot the poor devil five times!"

The cop said, "Now listen to me!
My handicap's down to a three.
I knew that this chap
had an eight handicap
so he had to get five shots from me!"

# Confidence

You take address position
your feet are shoulder wide,
lined up to the target,
elbows by your side.

You know you have it mastered,
it's a cakewalk so to speak.
There couldn't be a problem,
you've practised this all week.

You remember as you're placing
your thumb along the shaft,
that when you played your last shot
the other three all laughed.

It doesn't boost one's confidence
when the other three
think that where you're aiming
is the safest place to be.

# Lessons

He thought he'd pay for lessons,
he wanted to be taught
the things that all the Pros know,
the secrets of the sport.

He still goes 'round in fifty more
than anybody ought.
Now he thinks that lessons are
just a bloody rort!

There is no better use
of time than playing
the course well ... no
greater waste of time
than playing it badly.

# Cyril

Cyril said his handicap
(a modest 34 )
would best reflect his talent
were it scratch, or not much more.

There's little doubt it could have been
had it not been for
his ugly swing, atrocious putts,
weak grip, and massive score.

# Divine Assistance

It seems a simple pastime
this game of club and ball,
but one should be a genius
to take it up at all.

Scientists will tell you
it requires the sort of mind
that leaves old Albert Einstein
trailing miles behind.

A brain like a computer's
the most essential thing
to coordinate the ninety-eight
components of the swing.

To learn the Royal and Ancient's
fifteen thousand rules
requires a mental acumen
not bestowed on fools.

You memorise from magazines
the latest swing technique,
you get it right, then drop it for
the new one out next week.

You study golf instruction books,
a Herculean task;
perhaps the Lord could help you,
you'd only have to ask.

But you never go to church,
find praying little use;
your knees would never take it,
at least that's your excuse.

You say, "What me? Religious?
Most certainly I'm not!"
But find that while you're playing
you talk to God a lot.

# Ups and Downs

No one knows with putting
what it's all about.
There is no silver bullet,
you're either in or out.

One day, for no good reason,
it seems a piece of cake;
you have the feel for distance,
your eye can read the break.

You have the firm conviction,
you're mastering the sport;
your putts just keep on dropping,
like the shares that you've just bought.

Next day you find your judgement
of line and length so poor,
when attempting longer putts
it's best to cry out, "Fore!"

There is intense satisfaction
in knowing you look like a golfer:
the proper wardrobe, the state of the
art weaponry, the glasses, the glove ...
it's an illusion that lasts all the way
to the first tee.

# The Battler

Oh brave, resourceful weekend hacker,
determined, fearless pin attacker,
'tis only you that's man enough
to play a three wood from the rough.

Most ungainly of all swings,
elbows out like chicken wings,
you pop your head up, all abuzz,
to see it fly... it seldom does.

You know how bad your chipping's been
so putt from metres off the green.
Countless sad, appalling rounds,
out of luck and out of bounds.

You've never won a cup or prize,
all you get's the exercise.
You swear and curse, don't often cry...
play every week, but God knows why!

# Daly Tuition

I've followed John Daly forever,

bought his book, which wasn't so clever...

got smashed as a rat,

trashed my bedroom and that...

and my golf game's as hopeless as ever!

# Arnold

"A great par three!" said Arnold,
a proper golfing nut.
"I'll birdie this – a seven iron
and just a single putt!"

But Arnold badly duffed his drive,
it dribbled just a metre.
"I think this putt," his buddy said,
"will be a real WORLD BEATER!"

# Fashion

Angus is a steward;
you see him at the Open.
The sign he holds says, "QUIET"
it has officials hopin'
to introduce decorum,
silence rabble-rousers,
and any patrons half as loud
as Daly's latest trousers.

# His Royal Smugness

I knew when he rattled the pin,

he'd chipped from the trees and gone in.

Such a dead lucky break

was a bit hard to take,

like his bloody self-satisfied grin!

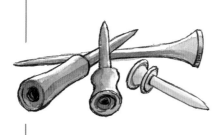

The trouble with getting birdies and pars is you're forever waiting on the tees.

# Hole In One

On our local golf course
is a pond that's very nice
but a bloody inconvenience,
to people prone to slice.

It's a bit more than a hectare
but centimetres deep;
is such a frequent hazard
to help you out they keep

a pair of rubber gumboots
just beside the edge,
so you can trawl your ball out
with a nine iron or a wedge.

The first time that I used them
I thought it rather fun,
but two steps in, quickly found,
I had a hole in one.

They always say a hole in one
is the epitome.
I'd have to say it didn't do
an awful lot for me.

# Stan

Stan and his wife
had a hobby for life,
they played every day as a two.
One day, on a whim
she jacked the game in,
exactly why Stan never knew.

The tipping point came
in the midst of a game,
she stormed off the course in a snitch.
As she managed to land
her approach in the sand,
she'd heard Stanley say, "Silly pitch!"

# Phil

Phil, a statistical nerd,

said to his mates, "Have you heard?

In world rankings my rating's

twelve million and eighteen

thousand nine hundred and third!"

# The Lost Ball

We slogged around the undergrowth
looking for his ball,
until he cried, "Well, here it is!
It wasn't lost at all!"

"Are you sure it's yours?" I asked.
"Certain!" he replied.
But his ball was in my pocket
so I knew he'd bloody lied!

# Bill

Bill and his wife
were having some strife
over how much he'd spent on his sub.
Not wanting a fight
on a Saturday night
he took her to dine at the club.

The steak was sublime,
the potatoes just fine
but the veges all flaccid and gritty;
in fact, such a mess,
he wrote to express
his thoughts on it to the committee.

He said in the letter
it should have been better,
far too much salt in the beans.
The committee wrote back
saying when they got flak
it was always to do with the greens.

# McEwan

Laird Ross McEwan
some puttin' was doin'
in the last of the day's fading light.
Said his man, Sean O'Hare,
"What ya have dere
is some borra, so putt to the right."

Countered Laird Ross
"I don't give a toss
if there be borrow or not,
for borrow, ye see,
does nae bother me...
I never pay back! I'm a Scot!"

# Tiger

As photographers crowded the tee,

Tiger yelled, "Please let me be!"

Why does he get

so bloody upset?

Photographers don't bother me.

# Awkward Lies

### THE UPHILL LIE
The ball above the feet.

### THE DOWNHILL LIE
The ball below the feet.

### THE BARE LIE
The ball on a grassless surface.

### THE BAREFACED LIE
The most difficult lie to pull off.

# Markers

There's an etiquette to putting:
it's your partner's turn to play,
but he can't putt because your ball
which missed is in the way.

You mark your ball with something
that won't impede his line,
something flat and fairly small,
a dollar coin is fine.

Just think how much cheaper
playing golf's become...
year's ago a dollar was
quite a tidy sum.

In fact it was a banknote
back in your father's day.
Before you could replace the ball
the thing had blown away!

# RIP

Fred, Bert, Stu and Arthur
were putting on the first,
when Fred dropped dead, the doctor said
his foofoo valve had burst.

"Fred's my bleedin' partner!
It isn't fair!" said Stu.
"There's no damned way that I should play
against the two of you!"

Said Bert, "There's four behind us,
we'll have to let them through
if we don't keep bloody moving...
let's get to Number Two."

As they toddled off the green,
Arthur, who was last,
went over to adjust the flag
and left it at half mast.

# Etiquette

There is a certain etiquette
to this ancient game.
Ignoring it will guarantee
approbrium and shame.

Four-letter words are frowned upon,
as everybody knows,
which seems a contradiction
as golf is one of those.

When someone hits their drive ten feet
with a dreadful shot,
"Tough luck!" is quite acceptable,
"Jeez, you're good!" is not.

Breaking wind is borderline,
permitted with the boys,
and okay in mixed foursomes
if it doesn't make a noise.

You'll be treated like a carrier
of leprosy or rabies
if you utter vulgar words
to do with making babies.

Another thing you must not do,
everyone tut-tuts,
is have your foot across the hole
while your opponent putts.

Any putting out of turn
brings forth such a moan.
It's easier and much more fun...
to play it on your own.

# African Stableford

A safari park owner called Brian

Holed in one with a number eight iron.

Then should have knocked off

Next hole he got scoffed

For lunch by a man-eating lion.

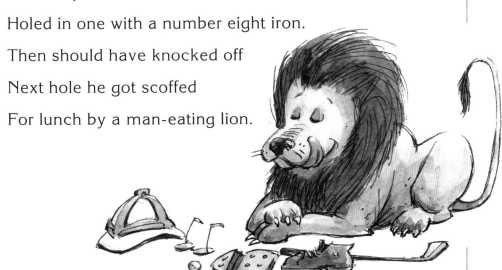

# McDiarmid

McDiarmid could nae sleep,
was twenty-five to four,
worryin' his puttin'
was ruinin' his score.

He rose and flicked the light on,
got his putter and a ball,
laid a tumbler on the rug
to represent the hole.

"Och aye! ya fool – now I'm awake!"
his wife Fiona said.
"Pop ya teeth back in that glass
and get back into bed!"

The amount of money
mankind spends on getting
into space is obscene, but
it's a fraction of that spent
annually on getting a small
ball from the top of a plastic
peg 400 yards into a hole
about the size of a coffee mug.

# McTavish

Duncan Ian McTavish,
Scottish hypocrite,
didn't hold with wasting time
but played golf quite a bit.

Slashing through the heather,
striding o'er the heath,
the thistles raked his sporran
and the ticklish bits beneath.

He'd slice like an old breadknife,
he'd hook a great amount...
and when he had an air shot
he'd cry, "That does nae count!"

Known for his native thrift,
not generous at all,
just like Adolf Hitler
he only had one ball.

He lost it down a rabbit hole
while chipping on the fen,
crawled in to retrieve it
and was never seen again.

When they took sad tidings
to the woman he had married,
She cried, "What luck! No bloody bill,
to have McTavish buried!"

# The Shark

I discovered in the game of golf
I'm not the fastest learner,
when I played a match against
that crafty pro Greg Turner.

I was on a sixteen
he was on plus two.
He said, "I'll grant a stroke a hole,
if that's okay with you?"

One hole to go, to my surprise,
we were, in fact, all square.
He said, "Let's make a special deal –
I'm sure you'll find it fair.
I'll give you two shots on this hole –
you're playing well you know –
if, before we've played it out,
I'm allowed one throw."

"You're on," I said, with confidence,
"sounds more than fair to me."
He landed on the green for two
and I was on for three.

Then he asked, "Do you recall
the throw that I can take?"
"Of course," I said... He took my ball
and threw it in the lake!

# Putting

There are so many putting styles,
at last count ninety-two.
Try them all and you will find
there's one ideal for you.

The one that I decided on
is number sixty-three.
Why I did, God only knows...
it's never worked for me.

# The True Believer

A sporting country vicar
with a wicked slice,
refrains from vile blaspheming;
too genteel and nice.

Only he, in wooded rough,
far from prying eyes,
knows that God is watching
so plays it as it lies.

They say the more golf one plays the better one gets. It doesn't work for me because each time I go out I play much more than I mean to.

# Golf vs. Rugby

Golf's a bit like rugby,
played in any weather,
but golfers know of hazards...
and don't all shower together.

# Paul

The problem was Paul
would lose a new ball
and occasionally two on each hole.
His mate saw no sense
in such needless expense
and assumed a congenial role.

He suggested to Paul,
"Hey, play an old ball
when your round's so incredibly bad."
Paul said,"Very good,
I would if I could,
but it's not something I've ever had!"

# The Addict

He's out there in all weather,
in rain or arctic gale,
the car park's underwater
but he turns up without fail.

He's lain awake all Friday night
rigid in the bed,
scoring countless birdies,
pars and eagles in his head.

The morning sky is black with rage
but that should blow away,
there's no capitulation...
he knows today's the day.

He scrubs his clubs to rid them
of all the grass and loam
he'd intended to clean off them
last time he brought them home.

His wife says, "In this weather?
Golf? You must be nuts!"
She doesn't know the ecstasy
of sinking twelve-foot putts.

He tees off in a southerly
that makes his front teeth ache
and splashes down a fairway
that's turned into a lake.

He makes it to the first green
and feels despairing when
he knows that had he got the putt
he'd have had an easy ten.

His brolly has turned inside out,
his shoes have sprung a leak,
he can't believe he's longed for this
all the bloody week!

# Neville & Matilda

Neville was a golf nut,
'twas the true love of his life,
until he met Matilda
and took her as his wife.

He thought they could share the game,
'twould be a blissful thing,
so took her to the golf course
to teach her how to swing.

In the first golf lesson
for which her husband took her,
she asked, "Why can't I hit it straight?"
He said, "You're just a hooker."

Not until that moment
had Neville ever thought
that golf could be a violent
and painful contact sport.

# Rodney

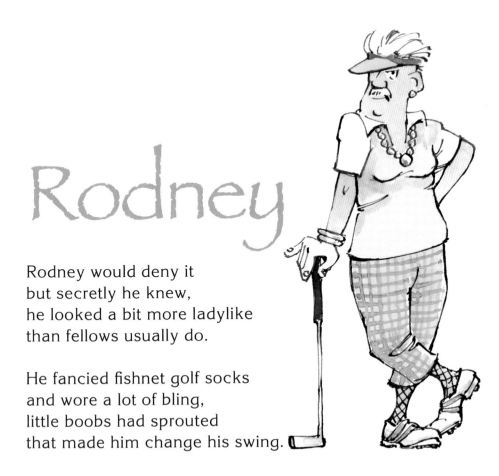

Rodney would deny it
but secretly he knew,
he looked a bit more ladylike
than fellows usually do.

He fancied fishnet golf socks
and wore a lot of bling,
little boobs had sprouted
that made him change his swing.

The doctor said that surgery
was something Rodney should
undertake without delay
to be a bird for good.

Poor Rodney said, "No, Never!"
which would've been a pity,
but changed his mind when summoned
before the club committee.

They said, "We have decided,
and everyone agrees,
if you have the operation
you can use the Ladies' Tees."

# Marital Bliss

On their joyous wedding night
he said to his new wife,
"Let's make a pact that we'll avoid
all argument and strife.

When e'er there's disagreement
and tempers start to fray
I'll scarper to the golf club...
hit practice balls that day."

For years he'd been on thirty-two,
had never won a match.
In just six months of marriage
he got right down to scratch.

You will hit your second shot
on a hole a whole lot further
if you play it quickly – while
you're still furious.

# The Affliction

You fly your drive out long and straight,
you know your luck is in.
Your silky smooth approach shot
stops two feet from the pin.
The putt is quite straightforward;
you mutter with a grin
"Such a classy birdie!"
and prepare to tap it in.

A gentle little practice stroke,
fluid, nice and slow,
address the ball and concentrate,
relaxed and primed to go.
Before you take the blade back,
a last look at the hole,
but the end point of your backswing
is the end of all control.

With knuckles white, frothing mouth,
a tightly clenched behind,
you lunge insanely at the ball
as if you've lost your mind.
You lurch about as though you've been
run down by a train
that's taken your composure
and a large part of your brain.

When the spasm's over,
you breathe again at last...
not only have you missed the hole,
you've dribbled twelve feet past.
You've dislocated both your wrists,
bitten through you lips
and left an eight-inch divot...
tough luck, you've got the yips!!

# Anniversary

A group of weekend golfers
coming to a green,
in the greenside bunker
found something quite obscene.

A geriatric couple
were struggling in the sand,
making love, despite the fact,
on golf courses it's banned.

The old chap said, "Excuse us,
we'll only be a minute…
'twas fifty years ago today,
right here, that we first did it."

"But why, back then," the golfers asked,
now rather red of face,
"choose a golf course bunker?
It's such a public place."

The man said, "Fifty years ago
'twas not a golfing course,
but a lovely field with buttercups,
and a rather startled horse!"

We got to know each other over a few holes.
"And what do you do?" he asked.
"Earthmoving," I replied.
"No, no," he said. "When you're not
playing golf…"

# Playing Through

On that rare occasion
you're really in the zone,
you're playing with a fluid swing
quite unlike your own.

You're getting lucky bounces,
(you prefer to call them clever)
and know that you're compiling
your lowest scorecard ever.

That's when the dawdling four in front
do what they're s'posed to do;
stand aside, hands on hips,
and ask you to play through.

It's then a game so easy
suddenly turns hard,
and bugger me, does guarantee,
one bad hole on your card!

# The Aussie

A coarse Australian golfer
said to his local Pro,
"The finer points of bunker play
are what I need to know."

The Pro said, "Play it firmly
but at a slower pace,
grip the club quite softly,
and open up the face."

The Aussie said, "I'm takin' in
all that you advise.
But when the face is open
I swallow lots of flies!"

# The Golf Fan

He'd saved up his dough
'cos he wanted to go
to see Tiger Woods play in the Masters,
but when he returned
had a terrible wound
on his elbow all covered in plasters.

He'd slipped on wet grass,
shattered his glass
and let out a blood-curdling howl...
arose from the mud
all covered with blood
which a caddy cleaned up with a towel.

Folk would implore,
"My God, that looks sore!"
He was not one for skiting or bluster,
but couldn't refrain,
just loved to explain
he had made the cut at Augusta.

# The Visitor

He pointed to the yellow pegs
and asked me, "What are these?"
He hadn't played our course before
and I said, "Ladies' tees."

There were four girls in front of us,
all cleavage and tanned legs.
He said, "They do! ... but tell me,
what are these yellow pegs?"

The greatest
satisfaction I know
is to hit a golf ball
really well ... long
and true. A close
second is throwing
a club into water.

# Mervyn & Ray

Mervyn and Ray
would play every day,
regardless of good or bad weather.
One particular day
Merv noticed Ray
had not got his golf game together.

Mervyn said, "Hey!
I've not seen you play
in such an incompetent fashion."
"The reason," said Ray,
I'm playing this way...
the wife's gone and cut back my ration."

"Don't agitate
yourself, me old mate,"
said Mervyn, rather discreetly.
"There are at least three
members, and me,
that woman has cut off COMPLETELY!"

Golf is insanely addictive –
by the time you've tried it,
it's already too late!

# Taking a
# Little Licence

If I'm playing golf alone
or with a friend, I find,
when I jot my score down
I tend to be quite kind.

When I score a struggling ten,
who could really mind
if I take some licence
and write it down as nine?

It has become a habit
I know that I'll get caught,
the day I get a hole in one
and write it down as nought!

Golf is the hangnail of
sport. You know it's going
to end in pain and tears
but you simply can't
leave it alone.

# The Duffer

As a true duffer
Trev had to suffer
ribald advice from his pals.
"Hey Trevor, old thing!
What a God-awful swing! ...
EVERYTHING moved but your bowels!"

Convinced they were wits,
they were tickled to bits
but discovered before very long...
when Trevor went red,
they knew what they'd said

was not only rude but quite wrong!

# Peter

A twelve handicapper called Peter,

missed a dead easy putt by a metre.

He was playing his wife,

the love of his life,

and who'd cook and clean if he beat her?

The thing that keeps one persevering is not so much the boundless optimism that it will all come right, but the gratification of occasionally seeing pros make mistakes and discovering that sometimes they can't do it either.

# The Address

It's really most important
how you address the ball;
not "Hello Sir or Madam"
I don't mean that all.

The way that you confront it is
the most important thing,
with both hands firmly intertwined
as you commence your swing.

Give the knees a little flex
as the body twists;
the hands throughout the backswing
never leave the wrists.

Next prepare for impact,
turning with your thighs:
to generate real club speed
tightly close the eyes.

Reopen them as you complete
your whirlwind follow-through.
If the ball's still sitting there
golf's not the game for you.

When I hit a promising drive and then shank a simple approach shot out of bounds, I take a really deep breath, look around me, and think what a lovely day it is ...

somewhere else!

# My Golf

More hits than the Beatles,
more chips than Burger King,
but I'm neither rich nor famous,
it's a most peculiar thing.

I've now compiled more hundreds
than Ponting at his best,
but never once been asked to play
in anybody's test.

I'm familiar with more bits of rough
than travellers far from home,
and know my head stays stiller
than your average garden gnome.

I know my set-up's perfect,
my grip is quite unreal,
my backswing's just like clockwork,
I've got timing, style and feel.

I bring the club down smoothly,
speeding up a tiny bit,
it's when the club gets to the ball
the whole thing turns to shit!

If I could do what Tiger does,
freeze and stop my swing,
just before I hit the ball,
now that would be the thing.

While the club is motionless,
the answer may well dawn ...
"Put the club back in the bag,
go home and do the lawn!"

As I put my clubs back in the
car, a fellow said, "Good round?"
"Brilliant!" I replied, with a sarcasm
lost on him.
"How many were you under?" he asked.
"How many WHAT? ... Trees? Rocks?
Bushes? Fairway mowers?"

# McKechnie

Angus Roy McKechnie
played golf every day,

but knew not why, exactly,
he couldn't really play.

In bouts of deep frustration
was often heard to say,

"If I was nae married
I'd give the game away."